Pebble®

Revised
and
Updated

Grandfathers

by Lola M. Schaefer

Consulting Editor: Gail Saunders-Smith, PhD

Capstone
press®

Mankato, Minnesota

Pebble Books are published by Capstone Press,
1710 Roe Crest Drive, North Mankato, Minnesota 56003.
www.capstonepress.com

Library of Congress Cataloging-in-Publication Data
Schaefer, Lola M., 1950–
    Grandfathers/by Lola M. Schaefer. — Rev. and updated.
    p. cm. — (Pebble books. Families)
    Includes bibliographical references and index.
    Summary: "Simple text and photographs present grandfathers and how they
interact with their families" — Provided by publisher.
    ISBN-13: 978-1-4296-1225-8 (hardcover)
    ISBN-10: 1-4296-1225-8 (hardcover)
    ISBN-13: 978-1-4296-1754-3 (softcover)
    ISBN-10: 1-4296-1754-3 (softcover)
    1. Grandfathers — Juvenile literature. 2. Grandparent and child — Juvenile
literature. I. Title. II. Series.
HQ759.9.S34 2008
306.874'5 — dc22   2007027095

Note to Parents and Teachers

The Families set supports national social studies standards related
to identifying family members and their roles in the family. This
book describes and illustrates grandfathers. The images support
early readers in understanding the text. The repetition of words
and phrases helps early readers learn new words. This book also
introduces early readers to subject-specific vocabulary words, which
are defined in the glossary section. Early readers may need some
assistance to read some words and to use the Table of Contents,
Glossary, Read More, Internet Sites, and Index sections of the book.

Printed in the United States   4964

Table of Contents

Grandfathers

Grandfathers are fathers
of mothers and fathers.

grandmother

mother

daughter

grandaughter

grandfather

Grandfathers
have grandchildren.

Busy Grandfathers

Grandfathers are busy.

Grandpa Fred

owns a bakery.

Grandpa George
builds bird houses.

Grandpa Les
goes for walks.

At Play

Grandfathers have fun.
Grandpa Lee
plays catch.

Grandpa Bill

comes to tea parties.

Grandpa Ed reads stories.

Grandfathers love
their grandchildren.

Glossary

bakery — a store or building where bread, cake, cookies, and other foods are baked in ovens

father — a male parent; your dad's father is your grandfather.

grandchildren — the children of a grandfather's son or daughter

mother — a female parent; your mom's father is your grandfather.

own — to have something that belongs to you; people who own businesses are in charge of that business.

Read More

Parr, **Todd**. *The Grandpa Book.* New York: Little, Brown, 2006.

Robertson, **J. Jean**. *Meet My Grandparents.* Vero Beach, Fla.: Rourke, 2007.

Internet Sites

FactHound offers a safe, fun way to find Internet sites related to this book. All of the sites on FactHound have been researched by our staff.

Here's how:

1. Visit *www.facthound.com*
2. Choose your grade level.
3. Type in this book ID **1429612258** for age-appropriate sites. You may also browse subjects by clicking on letters, or by clicking on pictures and words.
4. Click on the **Fetch It** button.

FactHound will fetch the best sites for you!

Index

Word Count: 49
Grade 1
Early-Intervention Level: 10

Editorial Credits
Sarah L. Schuette, revised edition editor; Kim Brown, revised edition designer

Photo Credits
Capstone Press, cover; Karon Dubke, interiors